Table of Contents

INTRODUCTION	1
What Does Marketing Success Look Like In a Digital, Social and Mobile Age?	3
Hit or Myth: Which Marketing Beliefs Are True?	9
How To Make People Curious About Your Brand.	12
The Suprising Math of Advertising Waste.	16
Eight Brand-Building Ideas for a Digital World.	19
When Are Brand Extenstions a Good Idea?	23
Suprising New Study on Facebook Marketing Effectiveness.	27
Shopper Path to Purchase: A New Approach to Media Planning.	30
What Marketing Research Needs to Learn From Behavioral Economics.	33
Four New Approaches To Segmentation in a Digital and Social Age.	37
Two Big Marketing Research Mistakes that Mislead Marketers.	41
Tooling Up For A Digital, Social and Mobile Age.	45
ABOUT	49

Introduction

Having started my blog over 5 years ago when I was Chief Research Officer at the Advertising Research Foundation, and continuing after founding my marketing and research consulting business (Rubinson Partners, Inc.) in 2010, I've now written about 100 blog posts as of September, 2013. I was surprised and gratified to see that the most popular blog post has been shared over 800 times and the top 10 blogs have been shared collectively about 6,000 times by all of you!

I regard my blogs as a dialogue. My writing them is a question to you, my readers, of how important is each idea and the problem it is addressing. The number of social shares is your answer. This "top ten" list is as much your creation as it is mine. You are the ones who find the best blog posts to share, often with your own interpretations and summary. Cool... teamwork!

Although my blog is called "Rubinson on Research", I alternate between blogging about marketing issues and research because I am trying to reinforce that these functions as well as web analytics can and must converge as never before in a digital age.

Think of the basic consumer-shopper circular process as people consume what they buy, deplete, then start planning their next trip; this results in a purchase and the cycle begins again. Before the advent of Google and social media, the only window into this process... brand consideration, preference, purchase and user satisfaction...was via surveys. Today we have constant signals as a natural byproduct of how people use digital and social media to shop and share thoughts about brands. The brands and retailers people search for and website visits give us a measure of brand consideration. Social media conversations give us a sense of brand perceptions and satisfaction. The volume of conversation and search suggest how much people care about your brand and are considering it for purchase. Frequent shopper data tells us what actually was bought and now, matching these datasets tells us if social media, digital ad exposure, visits to websites, etc. actually produce sales lift. Researchers not only want to listen for brand advocacy, marketers want to encourage it. The same activities create data that have both insights and marketing value.

More on this in the next section...

My blogs describing new fact-based insights, new ideas about digital, shopper, media strategies, discussing behavioral economics, and offering advice about marketing research methods are themes that underlie the most shared.

However, there is one common theme that ties these different topics together...

What Does Marketing Success Look Like In a Digital, Social and Mobile Age?

As I look at the top ten list, there is one question keeping both marketers and researchers awake at night that underlies just about every one of these top ten most shared blogs.

"What does marketing success look like in a digital, social, mobile (DSM) age"?

Marketers and researchers are playing catch-up ball...marketers are trying to catch up to consumers and researchers are struggling to catch up to the real time needs of marketers. Today, researchers still monitor brand KPIs that mostly come from brand tracking which largely follows the old model...survey-based, backward looking, slow, and continuing to reinforce a TV-first marketing culture.

CMOs compete with each other for who can appear the most progressive at embracing our digital, social, mobile world but the narrative is empty without evidence. Frankly, marketers know that earned media (conversations from consumers about your brand) and owned media (people visiting your brand on the web) are important but they just don't know how important relative to traditional media or promotion.

If marketers don't have a clear, cohesive picture of brand success in a DSM age, they will not be able to compete effectively and efficiently. And this picture must be validated by evidence and brands must be guided by aligned metrics.

The change in how people consume media is profound and marketing needs to adjust their beliefs on how to use media…paid, owned, and earned for brand-building. Researchers need to develop new metrics and ways of harnessing digital and social data to reflect this new worldview or risk becoming like the Encyclopedia Brittanica: great work made irrelevant by the cadence of digital society.

How The World Is Changing For Marketers:

From days of old…

In a traditional marketing era, marketers built brands largely based on running paid advertising to generate awareness, interest, desire, and hopefully action. In this worldview, consumers were not part of the media equation.

Marketers launched campaigns and waited to hear how successful they were. It was like playing football; run a play, be less than thrilled with the results, and then call time out to huddle up to decide what play to run next.

…to days of bold

In a digital, social, and mobile world consumers have become a significant part of the media process as they:

- Share, endorse or dissuade friends regarding branded content and their feelings about brands

- Lean-forward as they search, pull information, and seek opinions/ideas. For example, Google told me in an interview for one of my blogs that there are 8 BILLION searches in the US each month that are food recipe related.

- Join brand communities via Facebook, Twitter, signing up for e-mails, and downloading branded apps.

o And now, all of these actions can take place right at point of purchase and on the street corner via smart phones.

Now, best marketing practice is more like soccer; constant action requiring agility as you could be anywhere on the field at any point in time, but have a way to instantly sense and respond to the situation. Research systems need to move from backward looking, where we call timeout to assess the results to constant motion. The only way to do this is to bring digital and social data into the insights streams at near real time.

(Note: I use the "football-soccer" analogy that I first heard from my brilliant friend and colleague Wally Marx, describing how he was able to successfully launch Soft Soap and beat Procter, Colgate, Dial, and Unilever at the soap game.)

The Promise of Digital Measurement

Digital marketing offers the promise of being self-measuring and real time as consumers' self-directed digital behaviors (e.g. trademark search, branded app downloads), including social sharing, exposure to digital advertising and its effects, can be harvested and turned into KPIs. The relative passion that people have for brands, what they think of those brands and their sentiment are visible via social and digital data. No proprietary surveys are needed to gain quantitative evidence of the success of Old Spice, or how much more engaged people are with Starbucks (35 million Facebook fans) vs. Folgers (1 million Facebook fans) even though more people might drink Folgers every day.

Marketers must measure the progress of these brands using social and digital data streams, and not just use surveys. Furthermore, these new digital KPIs (Key Performance Indicators) of brand success represent the fusion of measurement and marketing action. If a KPI has to do with connections in social media (e.g. fans or followers) and your brand is weak on that metric, it immediately translates into a marketing action. If your level of trademark search is below that of competitors, you need to strengthen your content marketing strategies and optimize for search.

Challenges At Creating Digital Key Performance Indicators

No industry framework
Despite the promise, digital data are so abundant that without a framework, the data are overwhelming and chaotic. Currently, no comprehensive industry-accepted earned and owned media metrics actually exist yet (like GRPs and brand tracking guide TV advertising). As a result, the relative importance of paid, owned, and earned media is simply not known. Hence, there is a need for each advertiser to create a measurable model of what brand success looks like that will guide brands' digital, social, and mobile activities.

Data are deceptively hard to tame
Social media listening platforms are geared to mining conversations but need direction for measurement of owned media impressions as they either count a conversation as "1" (way undercounts) or as the number of followers of the author (way over-counts impressions). Facebook offers scores of metrics to page administrators so choices have to be made.

Digital display advertising can be measured by ad servers, tags, or by panels like comScore or Nielsen OCR and all have strengths and weaknesses…still the Wild West.

In frustration, advertisers often leave measurement decisions up to agencies but that creates chaos as agencies change across assignments.

Moving from Point A to Point B
Leaders need to do better. You must develop an ownable strategy for integrating naturally occurring digital and social data with survey data into your brand KPI and brand health approaches.

The need to integrate digital measurement around a comprehensive and contemporary view of brand success, one that translates insights into action in real time, is the biggest rock we have to move.

RUBINSON ON RESEARCH:
The Top Ten Blog Posts

Hit or Myth: Which Marketing Beliefs Are True?

(279 Social Shares)

Marketers are in a hunch business...making decisions whose effects will occur in the unknowable future. These hunches come from beliefs so when they are wrong, the results can be disastrous. Nothing is more important than solidly grounding these beliefs in evidence but sadly, they are too often grounded in mythology from stories that pundits tell built on faulty research, reinforcing each other, and giving the air of confirmation.

Take the 10 question Rubinson Partners "hit or myth" quiz!
(answers about the US market in the section below this)

HIT OR MYTH?

1. With over 30 million "likes" and only 2MM or so monthly visitors to Starbucks.com, people collectively spend more time with Starbucks content on Facebook than on the Starbucks website.

2. Over 20% of purchases in stores now come via showrooming, where people use apps to get the best price elsewhere while standing in the store.

3. By 2015, people will spend more time on the internet via their mobile devices than via their computers

4. Over 30% of time spent watching TV is timeshifted

5. There are over 1 Billion searches every month via Google for meal recipes

6. 90% of grocery shopping is on auto-pilot

7. TV advertising revenue is still growing despite the rise of digital advertising

8. Over 75% of those loyal to a brand in one year are loyal to the same brand the next year

9. People spend over $1 billion on virtual goods annually

10. Tablets take more usage time away from TV than from laptops

ANSWERS

1. Myth. People spend minutes per visit to owned media while very few fans revisit the fan page in a month and only seconds with updates on Facebook in their newsfeed.

2. Myth. 35% claim to do this but only a few percent actually showroom in a given month.

3. Hit. Smart phones will become the primary way we access the internet over the next few years. Are your brands mobile optimized?

4. Myth. 30% of people timeshift but it only accounts for less than 10% of TV viewing.

5. Hit. Google claims there are nearly 8 billion recipe related searches in a month. That is quite a role in the CPG path to purchase; are you aware and incorporating this?

6. Myth. As Kahneman says, people use System 1 (autopilot) until they encounter surprises. About 50% of purchase decisions are made in the store, so it is hard to say 90% are habitual auto-pilot purchases.

7. Hit. Yes, TV ad revenues continue to grow. Print is losing ad revenues, not TV.

8. Myth. 50% of those loyal to a CPG brand in one year are not loyal to that same brand in the subsequent year. My research while at NPD (contact me for a copy of the JAR article) and Catalina came to the same conclusion. I defined loyalty as buying the same brand 50%+ of the time and they defined loyalty as 75% share of requirements.

9. Hit. Amazingly, the market for virtual goods is huge. People give virtual gifts and use virtual currency to advance through game levels faster.

10. Myth. In surveys, people say that use of tablets is replacing use of laptops first and foremost. Tablets are a multitasking buddy to TV.

EXECUTIVE SUMMARY
Hit or Myth: Which Marketing Beliefs Are True?

Much of the narrative you read in Ad Age, MediaPost, eMarketer, or digital or social media companies is based on partial facts or faulty research and is simply not true.

Marketers are compelled to learn the facts. BTW, no industry leaders actually scored 100 on the quiz contained in this blog! Give it a try!

How To Make People Curious About Your Brand

(355 Social Shares)

"Curiosity is an emotion related to natural inquisitive behavior such as exploration, investigation, and learning, evident by observation in human and many animal species."
—Wikipedia

So What Does Curiosity Mean for Marketers?

Curiosity impels us to do things beyond functional need. It makes us explorers, discoverers. From shopper insights, we know that consumers like to browse, to discover new things. We purchase many (perhaps most) new products not because we arrive at the store with a perceived need for those particular items but, instead, because they're fun things we encounter as we shop. We're curious to try that new gourmet coffee, to unscrew the lid off of a shampoo bottle and take a sniff. Many shoppers love wandering around a Trader Joe's intending to find something interesting.

So marketers, take note: the curiosity impulse can lead people to discover and engage with your brand. When curiosity takes over there is no need to patiently move consumers through a linear funnel from awareness to interest to desire, blah blah. Curiosity leads to purchases that are serendipitous and often spontaneous. To leverage people's natural curiosity, consider the following strategies.

Build Curiosity Into Your Marketing Plans

• Create a brand experience that requires exploration and play. (Twitter, gaming and Bing— with the wonderful exotic photos– are three examples.)

- Create a stream of interesting new product forms. Air-freshener products are great at this.
- Create an offering that never stops surprising. iPhone apps, for instance, provide endless opportunities for discovery.

Building Curiosity Into Your Brand Communications

- Use both traditional and digital advertising to make people curious about your brand, and then send them to an owned-media digital destination for more. For an example, look no further than the Frito-Lay award-winning ad campaign that Ogilvy created for Cheetos: it used a variety of media to deliver people into "The Orange Underground," an imaginative, entertaining digital place that further whetted consumers' appetite for the snack food.
- Use teaser advertising for a major launch to build intrigue. For an active case in point, look at what Verizon used to pre-launch the new Android phones.
- Use massive multi-player games to build awareness—a practice well established by the movie and gaming industries.
- Use state-of-the-digital-art technology Augmented reality and QR codes will allow people to explore your brand in a retail setting like never before.

Build Curiosity By Retail Activation

For a retailer, curiosity equals exploration equals shopper excitement. Retailers always are struggling to create in-store excitement to engage shoppers to more fully navigate up and down the aisles.

- Create demo and tasting stations. People love to sample new foods; it combines curiosity with the strong attraction that people have to "free."
- Create thematic retail activation ideas that break the linear shelves (e.g., a party center; a "here's-what's-new-this-month" venue; an "essentials-for-less" destination, where any brand (including the store brand) that meets certain affordability guidelines gets secondary placement).

Herb Sorensen, author of Inside the Mind of the Shopper says that a typical supermarket carries some 40,000 SKUs but that a typical shopper buys 400 items in a year. Maybe part of the reason is that shoppers are out of ideas but would welcome new ones.

Shift Marketing Thinking; From Products to Experiences

To be interesting, you not only compete for attention with functional competitors, you go up against "unrelated" brands. Whole Foods (a retailer) competes in the mental marketplace of health/fresh with Dannon, Kashi (products), and Subway (restaurant). Whole Foods "competes" pretty well by building a sizable brand community across social media (e.g., more than 800,000 Twitter followers), having a wonderful blog and iPhone app about a wellness lifestyle with organic and fresh foods. Coke competes in social media such as Facebook and Twitter with Nike and with celebrities to be fanned and followed by consumers. Brands as experience is an important marketing concept. In a long-tail world of choices that are sometimes not very functionally different, perhaps "interesting" is the new "better".

EXECUTIVE SUMMARY
How To Make People Curious About Your Brand

Gets at the essence of the web experience that encourages users to instantly satisfy their curiosity by clicking a link and exploring something new. It is human nature to be curious and this blog suggests how marketers can make that work for their brands in a digital age going beyond TV-centric thinking brought over to digital.

The Suprising Math of Advertising Waste

(380 Social Shares)

John Wannamaker is famous for saying, "Half the money I spend on advertising is wasted; the trouble is I don't know which half." When I was Chief Research Officer at the ARF, I would often hear people say, "If only we could eliminate waste in advertising."

Being a curious soul, I decided to calculate how much wasted advertising a marketer can afford and still have a successful campaign. The advertising arithmetic will surprise you as it did me.

It turns out that, for a campaign to pay out, less than 1% of impressions need to be "impact impressions", that is, directly lead to a purchase. So stop bemoaning waste; accept it as part of an advertising calculus that leads to profitable brand building.

While this result is counter-intuitive (that's what makes it so interesting), the math is undeniable.

First, at a high level, consider the fact that a brand with even a modest ad budget is probably buying BILLIONS of ad impressions in the hopes of generating MILLIONS of unit sales. That already tells you that impact impressions can be a faction of one percent for the successful campaign.

Let's work through the numbers with a prototypical brand.
- The brand. 10% of US households buy it in a year and based on its price, repeat rate, purchase cycle and buying rate it annually generates 44MM unit sales and $110MM in dollar sales at retail.
- The action. It doubles its annual ad spend from $10MM to $20MM. At an average $5 CPM, this means they are buying an extra 2 BILLION impressions across various media.

- The expectation: Generate a 20% increase in sales which translates into about 2MM more households buying the brand and generating 8.8 MM in incremental unit sales.
- Impact impressions rate: Is a little less than one half of one percent which can be calculated as 8.8 million incremental units/2 billion impressions. Alternatively, we can think of the incremental advertising as generating about 2MM more buyers (who then make a stream of purchases) which makes the impact rate even smaller. As a logic check, we can also think of this as a 20% increase in sales for a doubling of ad spend, which is an ad elasticity of 0.20...on the high side but still within a mid-range of experience for existing brands.

Are the other 99% of impressions wasted? Not all are...they create consideration and familiarity from which a percent become new buyers, they reinforce beliefs and remind people of your brand as they are about to shop while competitors are still in consideration. But beyond that, I would advise against marketers thinking they can create such a rifle shot approach that we will ever be able to target the few percent of impressions that had an impact and save our money by not buying the "wasted impressions". I think that there is a huge amount of randomness in consumer and shopper brains so the great majority of those billions of impressions is needed to allow a small percent of new buyers scattered about (in targeting and brand perception spaces) to accidentally find the brand and begin buying it.

I do think that targeting will improve results but can never eliminate what people wrongly call waste. Even digital, where we can use the most sophisticated targeting analytics such as retargeting and lookalike modeling of conversions, achieves lifts in response that might be multiples of what we would get otherwise, but are still in the single digits. This means target but don't over target, or as Jack Wakshlag, Chief Research Officer at Turner says, "Segmentation is like salt. A little bit is good, a lot can kill ya."

Hopefully, working through the math has stimulated your thinking and reduced your anxiety about advertising waste, as it did mine. It will help you to reconcile the troubling industry narrative some put forth of how no one wants to watch ads on TV or click on them on their computer so marketers need an alternative to paid advertising. We now see how wrong that storyline is and the importance of focusing on sales impact to judge marketing effectiveness. Social and owned media are certainly part of a synergy but they amplify rather than replace the scale, power, and incredible affordability of using paid advertising channels.

EXECUTIVE SUMMARY
The Suprising Math of Advertising Waste

Building a simple mathematical model, I demonstrate that it takes only 1% of impressions to have a sales effect to create a campaign that pays out, or 99% waste sounds bad but is actually a good thing! Of course, reducing waste to 98% would be better as it would double ad response and some of the following blogs offer advice as to how to do this.

Eight Brand-Building Ideas for a Digital World

(422 Social Shares)

Technology is changing how we live our lives and the rules for brand-building. Here are eight ideas the agile brand marketer should consider.

Own something other than a feature

What does your brand own? Not just "stand for", but "own"? Is there something consumers associate with your brand and with NO OTHER brand? In this era when store brand quality is really good, the long-standing model of trying to differentiate based on product quality or unique features is not a sustainable strategy.

What you can own is your brand story, a personality, a community, a personage that brings the brand to life (like the "Dirty Jobs" guy and Ford), or most recently, the social media marketing success story that was launched with a superbowl commercial, the Old Spice guy. Zappos' brand is its culture and its culture makes it a unique entity in the marketplace. If you do NOT own something you are at risk of being de-listed by retailers...and if they don't carry you, shoppers can't buy you.

Bring your brand to life at retail

For many products, over half of purchase decisions down to the brand level are made in-store. Clever packaging, mobile apps, solutions-based shopper marketing all give you the opportunity to give your brand differentiated meaning at retail.

Listen to all the signals and then engage

People are talking about your brand. What are they saying? This will help you to align your vocabulary to consumers for marketing and marketing research purposes, and know what search terms to buy. Where are they saying it? A great case is Hennessy Cognac. They discovered high levels of traffic between their site and blackplanet.com. They found that people on blackplanet were interacting with and using the brand differently (e.g. more mixing). Ultimately, Hennessy took the brand in a completely different direction, "the global art of mixing" (full case in The ARF Listening Playbook)

Spend as much as possible on virtual audiences

A virtual audience is not an audience for a given media property; it is the collection of impressions and communications across properties and vehicles that can be delivered (or pulled) via digital media at exactly the right time, right place, right message, to the right person. For virtual audiences, the concepts of reach and frequency become less important as every "touch" has the potential for impact.

Some examples:

- Shopping apps like stickybits for smart phones allow you to bring a persuasive offer or message right to the point of purchase with sight, sound, and motion. Apps like Shopkick are location aware and can tell if you are in the store, triggering offers
- Screens at gas stations that advertise convenience store items
- Anything you can do in conjunction with search
- Re-targeting

Encourage people to interact with your brand beyond functional purpose

This will build attachment that differentiates your brand. Microsites (including Facebook pages) allow you to create gaming elements that can be turned into sharable assets. They allow customers to be heard, like "My Starbucks Idea". Rich media allows for interaction. Interactive TV is starting to emerge. Smart phone apps, owned media sites all give the opportunity for interaction and play.

Find a way to build a service component into your brand experience

This also builds attachment. Apple's genius bar is genius. On-star by GM/Cadillac was perhaps the first significant breakthrough of taking a product (a car) and finding a way to give it a service dimension. You don't just buy a Gevalia coffee maker, you join a club that offers shipments of coffee to your home. Adding service to your product builds constant involvement and also gives you additional monetization opportunities.

Simplify people's lives

We live in a world that is potentially overwhelming. There are 40,000 SKUs in a typical supermarket. We have hundreds of TV channels to choose from, and that is a tiny percentage of the number of websites we might be interested in visiting. We are bombarded with thousands of brand messages every day. Consumers use rituals and heuristics to simplify their life (think of how the first 30 minutes of your day is probably on auto-pilot).

For example, manufacturers partner with retailers to improve store shoppability, that is, making it as easy as possible for shoppers to find what they are looking for, to find solutions, and to navigate the store as efficiently as possible.

Monitor all signals of what brand success looks like in a digital age

The sensing of brand success has gotten much more complex as signals exist in many more places. Your insights team needs to collate all of these signals into a cohesive picture. Brand sales and tracking data are still important, but what are people saying about you in social media? What are you hearing from customer care? How many fans do you have to your Facebook page?

EXECUTIVE SUMMARY
Eight Brand Building Ideas for a Digital World

Offers ideas that could never be implemented before digital that cut to the heart of why content marketing is so important.

The key thought here is to realize your brand/consumer relationships need to go way beyond functional purpose and that you must compete for thought leadership with functionally unrelated products regarding a lifestyle, a health concern, etc.

When Are Brand Extensions a Good Idea?

(477 Social Shares)

Line extensions (e.g. a new flavor of Crest toothpaste) and franchise extensions (e.g. Crest Whitestrips®) are thought to be more affordable ways to introduce new products and have a higher success rate vs. creating completely new brand names. In this recessionary "do more with less" marketing era, brand extension strategies for new products become increasingly alluring.

However, brand extensions are not always a good idea. Through the years, I have been involved with forecasting the sales potential of hundreds (maybe thousands) of line and brand extensions and wanted to share what I think are some important insights.

Insight #1—a brand extension strategy for launching a new product only works if your existing brand has high enough parent brand penetration.

The success of a brand extension has much to do with pre-existing brand equities as it does with the characteristics of the new items.

In the early 80s, General Mills launched a new flavor of Cheerios called "Honey Nut Cheerios". Concept test results were good but not off the charts yet when this new flavor was launched, it got an unpredictably high level of purchase trial given its modest advertising and promotion budget.

When I analyzed actual in-market results regarding trial rates for Honey Nut Cheerios and many other line extensions separately by those who bought the parent brand buyers vs. non-buyers, I found that parent brand buyers had a 2-6X HIGHER trial rate (e.g. 18% trial among parent brand buyers vs. 3% among non-buyers). Furthermore, it was only partially explained by higher purchase intent. The big factor was that the conversion of positive purchase intent into trial among parent brand buyers was much higher. In fact, the knife cut both ways; people who did not buy your brand were LESS likely to try the new line extension relative to their stated purchase interest than if it had a new brand name. Hence, overall trial for your new brand is the mixture of trial rates (one much higher, one a little lower), weighted by what percent of households buy your existing brand. It's easy to envision that there is a tipping point that denotes when your parent brand is big enough that a brand extension approach makes sense to consider.

Insight #2—Brand extensions that are not connected with the meaning of the base brand are destructive even though they might hit year one sales targets.

If you launch brand extensions that don't reinforce the parent brand image you might be turning your brand into a Frankenstein's monster of spare parts. That's why naming Spaghetti Sauce "Prego" rather than "Campbell" or calling a premium line of autos "Lexus" rather than "Toyota" made so much sense. It's also why I question Starbuck's instant coffee. What the marketer thinks is a brand extension the consumer might not view the same way. Here is how you can tell. In concept testing, if positive purchase interest towards the new product isn't at least 30% higher among parent brand vs. non-parent brand buyers that means that your buyers are not seeing the connection between the new product and your existing brand. This is a warning sign that, while the sales potential for the new product might be acceptable, unconnected products will share the same brand name.

Insight #3—Emphasize brand-building (e.g. advertising, social media) to build the master brand and shopper marketing and couponing to sell the brand extension.

The key point is that line extensions are bought out of preference for the brand and acceptability for the line extension, not preference for the line extension.

An extension of a brand someone buys enjoys instant credibility because users trust anything they connect with that brand. For new flavor and size line extensions you might not need anymore than to be visible in the store or offer a coupon. Because line extensions are bought out of acceptability, there is random component to whether they buy it or not. Therefore, the more SKUs your brand already has, the lower the trial rate will be among your own parent brand buyers.

Marketers want to use brand extension strategies as much as possible today because it is a more affordable way to introduce products but the key is having enough rocket fuel, i.e. brand equity, to get the rocket (i.e. brand extension) off the ground.

EXECUTIVE SUMMARY
When Are Brand Extentions a Good Idea

Most of new product launches are really brand extensions so it is important to understand that the rules are different than for launching new brands. I have a lot of experience here from creating the first line extension forecasting model in the industry and share my knowledge in this blog.

Suprising New Study on Facebook Marketing Effectiveness

(517 Social Shares)

I was invited to present at Wharton's Future of Advertising project, empirical generalizations II and choose to focus on the brand impact from Facebook. I partnered with Compete, Inc. leveraging their panel of 2MM for this analysis.

The first thing to note is that my assumption about people who like a brand on Facebook already being predisposed to that brand turned out to be true. They are 8X more likely to already be interacting with the brand's website vs. non-fans. This creates an analytic challenge, because you need to control for this in determining if liking a brand on Facebook CAUSES any increase in value to the brand, otherwise you will way overestimate the impact.

We studied 63 brands across 4 months in beauty, food/restaurant, and retail (sectors where sessions on owned media lead directly to sales). This is the first study that precisely measures the effect of liking a brand as it looked at the same person's clickstream behavior towards a brand for 30 days before and 30 days after they liked that brand.

So here is what we found.

There IS, in fact, an 85% lift in the number of sessions on a brand's website within 30 days of becoming a fan of a brand on Facebook. Liking a brand on Facebook DOES matter. However, the effect all comes from the small subset who return to the fan page. For them, there is a four-fold increase in their visits to that brand's website after liking the brand. Likers who did not return exhibited virtually no increase at all in website visits.

Our study also found that those returning to the brand page tend to be a small percentage of fans so the overall impact on brand website sessions is modest under current marketing approaches.

The fact that a second visit to the brand page is needed to create impact suggests that Facebook social impressions in a fan's newsfeed have little impact beyond their role in encouraging a return visit to the fan page. The inferences I draw from this is that every Facebook brand newsfeed update should offer a reason for a fan to go back to their brand fan page and the page itself should encourage stickiness.

"This research clearly indicates that marketers must be focused on not only increasing the number of total fans, but on driving repeated interaction with the fan page. It is this repeated interaction that leads to measurable lifts in visitation to owned media properties", says Mike Perlman, Vice President of Agency & Publisher Solutions at Compete.

This research also has importance measurement implications. It supports the need for a metrics approach I have trademarked called "Tyme with brand" ™ that is intended to measure the patterns and quantity of time that people spend with a brand, going beyond the gross number of impressions that marketers get via social media. If you do not measure tyme with brand, a marketer will certainly overestimate the importance of social media vs. owned media.

EXECUTIVE SUMMARY
Suprising New Study on Facebook Marketing Effectiveness

Clearly understanding the value of a Facebook fan is at or near the top of the list for marketers. I was honored to work with Compete to conduct one of the most comprehensive studies of this, across nearly 70 brands. The results were surprising ...yes, Facebook fans are quite valuable but only if you get them to revisit your Facebook page!

Shopper Path to Purchase: A New Approach to Media Planning

(690 Social Shares)

Media planning relies on two main approaches for shaping media strategy:

- Media habits approach: How does a marketer's target consumer spend time with media and specifically, which media properties are "target rich" environments? For example, online publishers often use a media habits argument to explain why they should get a share of ad dollars that is closer to share of media time.
- Touchpoints influence approach: Services like Integration or Compose are centered on self-reported approaches to prioritize which brand communication touchpoints influence someone's brand choice regarding a particular type of product/service or in conveying a certain brand benefit.

Let me add a third approach to the mix that comes from the field of shopper insights that would have a big impact on the allocation of media spending.

- "Path to purchase" approach: Understand the journey by which shoppers come to buy a particular brand, product, or service. Did they decide before or after entering the store? Did they do research as they started their shopping process? How did they research their purchase? What are the media touchpoints that best map to each leverage point in the path to purchase process?

Understanding "Path to Purchase" will change marketing and media priorities. In most cases, it is likely to increase the budget for search, comparison shopping, and particularly in-store shopper marketing vs. using a media habits approach because those places don't have a big share of media time but they are where the "lean-forward" action is. Shopper insights research shows that, for many products, 50% or more of purchases and brand choices are decided on right in the store. For such products, to put it in terms that media planners can relate to, shopper marketing is like recency on steroids.

The touchpoints influence approach might miss the mapping of a touchpoint to a brand objective. Brand teams should have two broad classes of communication goals: creating and maintaining desired brand meaning, and reminding people of the brand as close to the decision point as possible (recency). If different touchpoints best map to specific marketing goals, the logical implication is that impressions and "reach points" across media platforms are not interchangeable or additive; this suggests that multi-platform reach calculations, a main purpose of media habits studies, become more of a media insight than a quantitative measure needed for creating a media plan.

A more important media calculation might be to create meaningful recency and "likelihood to see/hear" (LTS)factors for different media. For example, in comparing TV to shopper marketing, TV might have a higher LTS factor (20 or so commercials in a show vs. 40,000 SKUs in a grocery store) but a lower recency factor vs. advertising that is right at the point of purchase. Hypothetically, cinema advertising might have the highest LTS of all touchpoints (you're sitting in the theatre waiting for the movie to start) but a really low recency factor. However, the recency factor itself might be less important when marketing's main objective is "imparting brand meaning" (say during the launch of a brand).

EXECUTIVE SUMMARY
Shopper Path to Purchase: A New Approach to Media Planning

Understanding "Path to Purchase" will change marketing and media priorities. It will increase emphasis on both paid and organic search, display advertising on sites that are visited when researching a purchase in that category, behaviorally targeted digital advertising when someone is tagged as shopping for a certain type of product/service and particularly in-store shopper marketing. This is one of the most important considerations to add to media planning that will turbocharge the ROI of marketing spend.

What Marketing Research Needs to Learn From Behavioral Economics

(694 Social Shares)

Behavioral Economics is the study of how people make decisions. It turns out we are not the coldly rational Vulcans that economists once thought we were. We think with our emotions. We are subject to giving different answers to the same questions asked or framed a little differently. We are risk-averse leading us to walk away from a better deal, and overly attracted to short-term reward. We use simple heuristics (Herb Simon's concept of bounded rationality) based on only a few considerations to make decisions that are "good enough" rather than trading off every possible feature (think about that the next time you ask for brand ratings on 30 attributes!) Behavioral economics lives at the crossroads of economics, cognitive psychology and anthropology in order to understand decision-making that is filled with the shortcuts we all use and of which we are only partially self-aware.

Marketing research needs to put a little behavioral economics in its game.

Nudge the respondent. Professor Dick Thaler's best-selling book "Nudge" is all about the idea that there is no neutral way to frame choices. "...simply by rearranging the cafeteria, Carolyn was able to increase or decrease the consumption of many food items by as much as 25%. Carolyn knows she can increase consumption of healthy foods..." The conclusion: Carolyn is a choice architect and there is no such thing as a neutral design.

Aren't research teams constructing surveys also choice architects? Survey-taking is chock full of decision-making. Should I join this panel? Should I click on that link? Even answering survey questions involves decision-making because people are not opening "a container" and just letting truthful answers pour out of their heads. They are reconstructing memories and opinions in the context of their current mental state, how the question is framed and asked, and how the preceding parts of the survey have brought a respondent to the next question. Brand equity research systematically understates preferences for store brands. Perhaps we should be willing to bend research "rules" to help people access their true feelings and preferences for lower priced alternatives?

Heat up the respondent. We tend to study preferences at times that are divorced from a respondent being in a need state. Noted Behavioral Economist George Lowenstein might caution us against this. He describes his research on cold-hot empathy gaps as follows:

"A ... focus is on people's predictions of their own future feelings and behavior. ...when people are in a cold state–i.e., not hungry, sexually aroused, in pain, angry, etc.–they underestimate the impact of such "visceral" (hot) states on their own future behavior. "

From a research protocols point of view, this leads me to wonder if current concept testing does enough to "put people in the mood" especially if the idea is innovative.

Reflect the decision heuristics people use. Except for shopper insights research, we researchers tend to study preferences for things rather than the decision process that people go through. We need to study both. Gerd Gigerenzer (his work was heavily referenced in Gladwell's book Blink) talks about "simple heuristics that make us smart". What heuristics is the shopper using? I hypothesize that shoppers sub-consciously use a satisficing strategy to make a shopping trip less laborious. They are intuitively rank-ordering choices and taking the first alternative starting at the top of the list that is good enough, that meets their criteria. This might explain why a highly preferred brand is not always bought; it takes BOTH brand meaning AND activation to result in a purchase.

Create social contracts. Another important insight comes from Dan Ariely's book, "Predictably Irrational" about social vs. monetary contracts. A few years ago, they studied a day care center in Israel to determine whether imposing a fine on parents who arrived late to pick up their children was a useful deterrent. Before the fine was introduced, the teachers and parents had a social contract, with social norms about being late. Thus, if parents were late — as they occasionally were — they felt guilty about it — and their guilt compelled them to be more prompt in picking up their kids in the future. But once the fine was imposed, the day care center had inadvertently replaced the social norms with market norms. In other words, since they were being fined, they could decide for themselves whether to be late or not, and they frequently chose to be late. Needless to say, this was not what the day care center intended.

The ARF hypothesized implications for incentivizing respondents to join panels and take surveys. The Foundations of Quality research proved that those who are motivated by a social contract (i.e. giving my opinion is the right thing to do) rather than receiving cash incentives exhibited more diligent survey taking behavior.

A behavioral economist might offer, "It's not your survey that's a delicate instrument, it's the human mind!" The challenge to producing consistent and reliable marketing research data goes well beyond sample representativeness. We need to think more like Behavioral Economists.

EXECUTIVE SUMMARY
What Marketing Research Needs to Learn From Behavorial Economics

Behavioral economics, the study of how people make decisions, is a hot area and I apply it to marketing research practice as survey-taking is chock full of decision-making. Survey questions involves decision-making because people are not opening "a container" and just letting truthful answers pour out of their heads. They are reconstructing memories and opinions in the context of their current mental state, how the question is framed and asked, and how the preceding parts of the survey have brought a respondent to the next question. By becoming better choice architects, we can address habitual biases such as understatement of buying store brands.

Four New Approaches To Segmentation in a Digital and Social Age

(733 Social Shares)

Traditional consumer segmentation can be maddening. It is at the heart of marketing practice to group consumers into segments based on their needs and self-stated psychographic profiles and to then attempt to target a high priority segment with new offerings and advertising. Yet, it simply does not work that well because it is rarely very actionable.

I remember once conducting a massive new product forecasting study where we were asked to put segmentation questions into the study. There was virtually no difference in purchase intent across the segments! Tell me again how this segmentation helped with innovation?

Remember Best Buy's commitment to customer centricity? The segments simply did not lead to impactful redesign of their stores.

Take an attitudinal segment and try to target them on analogue TV. You often wind up looking at demographic indices for that segment to place media which turns the rifle shot into a scattershot. OK, you hit the mark but you hit a lot of other targets too. And, while I am airing our marketing research dirty laundry, have you ever tried to score the same people into attitudinal segments at different points in time? My experience suggests that you will probably only classify 50-60% into the same segment.

Jim Stengel, the former CMO at Procter said at a conference in October 2012, "Get close to the consumer and do something with it". In segmentation, marketing research never seems to get to the "...do something with it" part

...but here's how that can change.

Segment moments. I am much more interesting to Ford or General Motors when I am looking to buy a car then right after I make the purchase, am I not? I happen to be on a diet now which makes me much more interesting to Atkins, Dukan and Weight Watchers than I was a month ago. Moments segmentation is better for innovation and for media strategy intended to influence the path to purchase. In a digital and social age, moments become directly targetable because I, the consumer, do things differently on my self-guided tour of the internet depending on my current goals, giving out forensic signs. I seek out different content, I search for different terms, I like different things on Facebook, and different products show up on my frequent shopper data. All highly targetable without needing to water things down with demographics. (For an example of moment segmentation on understanding smart phone use and motivations, click here.) (The supplier was InsightsNow, Inc., I was the consultant, and AOL and BBDO were the clients.)

Segment for ad targeting based on brand loyalties. Increasingly, we can merge digital and social data with frequent shopper data for ad targeting. (Facebook just cut a deal with Datalogix to do this for example.) Rentrak and TRA have each merged TV viewing with frequent shopper data. The "so what" is that a marketer can now target their advertising to "switchables". Who are they? The consumers who buy your brand occasionally but not most of the time. You will find a much higher response to advertising and promotions from switchables than from those who are completely loyal to either you or some competitive brand.

Segment people as shoppers. Do I plan purchases or decide in store? Do I like to explore to find new meal ideas? Do I like to sample the gourmet cheeses? Do I like to sniff the fragrances of air fresheners and shampoos? Do I probably have an infant at home given diaper and formula purchases? All of these have clear action implications for category adjacencies, store layouts, and specific shopper promotions delivered in a customized way, increasingly via mobile apps. Is there a consumer attitudes segmentation that can claim the success of what DunnHumby did for Tesco in the UK? Not that I know of.

Segment people based on targetable interests and values. Rather than create a psychographic battery of questions for segmentation and HOPE that we can target segments, why not flip this around? Why not analyze the interests, cultural values, and lifestyle characteristics that are available via Facebook or Google profiles and create segments on factors that reflect those actionable characteristics? That way, you can take your segmentation and do something with it! Furthermore, every ad campaign becomes a test that you have the segment right that you are targeting because they should exhibit greater response.

Final point. Traditionally, marketing research seeks to create a small number of segments that each represent sizable opportunities. This is still important for motivating innovation ideas, but when it comes to ad targeting, you can have many micro-segments as advertising is micro-targeted…served up one impression at a time in search, and with real time exchanges.

EXECUTIVE SUMMARY
Four New Approaches to Segmentation in a Digital and Social Age

Segmentation is at the heart of marketing, yet we rarely create segments that are actionable. The digital age can change all that. Here are four approaches that produce media targeting strategies, guaranteed to be actionable based on segmenting moments (hyper relevance), segmenting loyalties (switchables), segmenting shopping patterns (shopper marketing), and segmenting lifestyles (social and publisher targeting).

Two Big Marketing Research Mistakes that Mislead Marketers

(833 Social Shares)

Book authors, trade journal reporters, consulting firms, and influential bloggers can fill marketing teams' heads with some really bad ideas. As these stories reverberate around the echo chamber, they seem to confirm each other and voila, a wrong belief becomes entrenched. Examples: pundits' predictions 5-10 years ago about TV's demise were wrong. Current scare tactics about showrooming appear equally flawed.

Usually, this starts with a bad marketing research mistake turned into a compelling narrative. The two classes of marketing research mistakes I want to focus on here are:

1. Confusing incidence with market share
2. Asking questions that people cannot answer

Confusing incidence with market share

The incidence of people who ever engage in a disruptive activity can really scare marketers. For example, it appeared that TV will soon be dying when you looked at the percent of people who watch video online or watch timeshifted TV on their DVR and presumably fast forward through commercials. However, when you look at SHARE of viewing minutes, you get a completely different story. From a Nielsen cross platform report in Q1, 2011, we see that the incidence of watching shows on a timeshifted basis was about a third of TV viewers but it only accounted for 6% of viewing minutes. About half of people watched video on the internet but it accounted for less that 5% of minutes. As with food, light snacks rarely replace full meals.

Now let's turn to an issue getting lots of press these days, showrooming. This is the phenomenon that people walk into a Best Buy or Walmart, for example, see what they want to buy but then actually buy it from another online retailer via their mobile app, often via Amazon. This is so scary that Best Buy is even creating new store formats to combat this. A study by comScore in April 2012 shows that 35% of respondents claim they have showroomed. However, how MUCH are they doing this? A joint study by IDC and Onavo (who has a metering solution for app usage) reports that key price comparison shopping apps are only used by 1-3% of iPhone users an average of 2 times per month. A study reported on in Mediapost adds that about half of showrooming leads to purchases in that same retailer physically or online. Incidence of showrooming? Scary! Share of purchases diverted by showrooming? Still really low single digits.

Asking questions people cannot answer

Recently I was reading the revised edition of "Eating the Big Fish" (Morgan, Adam; 2009-04-03), a highly regarded marketing book but I was quite disappointed with the bad survey data it used as the setup for the book's recommendations.

- Survey study by Yahoo and OMD in 2006 showed people spend 2 ½ hours per day on TV but 3.6 hours/day on the internet.
o The only problem is that these data bear no resemblance to reality. Nielsen is the gold standard for TV viewing measurement and people actually watch about 5 hours per day of TV and access the internet a fraction of that time.

o Annoyance with TV Advertising is increasing.
- This is a bad question. Are movie trailers annoying which are really just long commercials? I bet not. Does this mean the effectiveness of TV advertising is declining at driving sales? Not from the analysis I did in 2009 of 388 commercials ROI assessments. In fact, that study was the basis of Dave Poltrack (Chief Research Officer at CBS calling Forrester's predictions bullsh*t at an ANA conference. Please read the article and listen to the soundbite.

One of the worst marketing research abuses I have seen, supporting that a tsunami of showrooming was coming, was reported on in Mediapost where the study asked consumers about retailing practices they expect to see by 2020. Really? People are concerned about stretching their food dollars to the next paycheck and marketers are abdicating their responsibilities for directing a company's future by just asking consumers straight out about showrooming in 2020? See how one bad story can reinforce the other in the echo chamber?

This blog is not an indictment of marketing research. In fact, it is the opposite; it is a statement of the importance of basing marketing beliefs on grounded insights from marketing research executed in a world class way. Let us shift marketing research back to the professionals and let's not break some simple rules.

EXECUTIVE SUMMARY
Two Big Marketing Research Mistakes That Mislead Marketers

Pundits compete in the echo chamber for thought leadership, often fueled by bad marketing research designed to feed a false narrative. The two classes of marketing research mistakes I focus on here are:

1. Confusing incidence with market share
2. Asking questions that people cannot answer

For example, the percent who have ever checked a price on their smartphone while standing in a store (showrooming) is high; the percent of transactions affected is low single digits. Compound this with a survey question about how likely you would be to buy via your smartphone while standing in a store by 2020 (yes, someone did this) and you have a myth.

Tooling Up For A Digital, Social and Mobile Age

If you want to manage it, (or if you're a media company, 'sell it') you need to measure it.

Metrics need to:

1. Be aligned with the new vision of how to build brand success in a DSM age
2. Offer a complete picture of brand success (in other words, if the arrows on your dashboard are all pointing up, the brand must be headed up as well)
3. Be unambiguous (both easy to understand and not be subject to competing explanations when they move)
4. Provide protocols owned by the client that are repeatable, automate-able, and documented so any agency or supplier can follow the client's way of doing things
5. Be driven by underlying data streams, warehoused in a way that serve modeling, campaign tracking, and brand KPI purposes
6. Offer near real time feedback so campaigns can become fast-pivot for in-flight optimization

And this means that marketing research needs to overhaul the metrics they have relied on. The old school survey metrics of brand awareness, brand equity, attribute ratings, etc. while they might still have value, are simply incomplete to measure what the lean forward marketer is trying to accomplish.

Here are some critical metrics to equip you for a DSM age.

1. Metric one: Paid, owned and earned impressions

Marketers and agencies use this phrase but few have measurement strategies in place. Marketers need to know, "In total, are we increasing the amount of communication presence about our brand?"

o   What it takes:
•   Paid: advertising the marketer pays for. (Protocols for digital impressions will need to be established. How are you capturing viewable impressions, for example?)
•   Owned: pageviews from visits to a marketer's website (readily available via web analytics, e.g. Google Analytics, that the website team gets). Include impressions that arise from showing up on the first page of organic search results and branded app sessions.
•   Earned: you will not get a perfect view of this, so you need to just set some rules for repeatable methods for measuring this. Do NOT use the total number of followers of those commenting about your brand, as some do, as that will over-count the number of earned impressions (since the probability that a given follower or fan sees a given comment is actually very low because people are on Twitter and even Facebook for only minutes per day). Make sure you include the number of post impressions from your Facebook brand page updates; this is certain to be the largest source of earned impressions if you have built a sizable following.

2. Metric two: CPM—cost per thousand for all impressions, where we include owned and earned impressions

o   If a marketer does not pay for owned and earned impressions, the possibility exists to reduce your average CPMs if the percent of impressions that come from consumer generated sources increases. Are we experiencing an increase in consumer generated impressions?
o   What it will take: take your media costs and divide them by all impressions (paid, owned, earned as defined above).

3. Metric three: Tyme with brand ™.

o   Some impressions gain fleeting attention, and some (like owned media visits) generate substantial time that people spend with brands, enabling the brand to convey its meaning.

o   What it will take. Again, there is no perfect measurement approach but you can create repeatable rules. The main components are social media conversations, owned media visits, display ad views, and video commercials either on TV or online. Time spent on owned media visits can be directly measured via web analytics and you will be surprised how much more time with brand this contributes vs. social media does. For social media conversations and display ad views, a comScore executive suggested that 1 second per exposure is reasonable but the marketer may wish to conduct a one time foundational study to assess this. Video views online can be directly measured. TV will be the main source of time for most brands. I suggest that you assume (or conduct a foundational study to get at) a normative rule of the percent of commercials that are seen at all and the percent of the commercial that is seen. Even if this results in assuming that 5% of the 30 second commercials are seen, the number of impressions delivered via TV advertising is so massive, that this will be the number one way that people spend time with brand in terms of media touchpoints, perhaps even rivaling product use time.

4. Metric four: Community size.

o   Consumer marketers always had an anonymous relationship with consumers whose identity was never known. Not anymore. In social media and via websites, people can now "join" a brand. This creates a powerful one-to-one marketing opportunity. The reach of this marketing opportunity is determined by the size of the community you have built.

o   What it will take: add together the number of Facebook fans, Twitter followers, those who have signed up for e-mails, subscribed to content, downloaded your branded app, etc. Grow this installed base of fans over time.

5. Metric five: Social sentiment and brand meaning.

Sentiment refers to a score of how positive or negative social media comments about your brand are. Brand meaning refers to what benefit and value connections a brand stands for. Brand meaning can be monitored from social media conversation and from attribute ratings in brand trackers.

6. Metric six: Conversions.

The web offers all marketers a unique opportunity that only direct marketers had before; the ability to track the impact of a marketing communication on an individual consumer and determine return on marketing in a very precise way. On the web, you can track the impact of advertising on acts that have value to you, even if you do not sell products online. Call these actions, "conversions". For example, Kraft might not sell much product online but if anyone downloads or prints a recipe from kraftrecipes.com, that can be considered a conversion...it clearly raises the probability that Kraft items called for in the recipe will be bought. These conversions can be related back to marketing actions so the impact of different digital efforts can be assessed and marketing dollars can be moved around in-flight.

- What it takes: classify a set of actions as conversions and built conversion code into these pages (there are various ways of doing this, such as imbedding a conversion pixel into a thank you page.) Relate these conversions to cookies on the user's browser that mark their exposure to a display ad or e-mail. Also, you can relate conversions to sources of traffic (search—which terms, direct traffic, coming from clicking on an ad, coming from a particular domain). For example, if you knew that conversions were being driven in a persistent way over time from a particular search term, you would want to buy variants of those terms in search engine marketing and make sure that your website offers content that leads your brand to show up in organic search results.

About Rubinson Partners, Inc.

Joel Rubinson
President of Rubinson Partners, Inc.

- Rubinson Partners, Inc. (RPI) was founded in 2010 by the former Chief Research Officer at the Advertising Research Foundation
- Clients include leading marketers, marketing research firms, and digital media companies.
- Founder was the Chief Research Officer at the ARF, 25 years as chief research officer at The NPD Group, Advanced methods practice leader for Vivaldi (leading branding consultancy), and head of analytics in North America and global lead on shopper insights for Synovate.
- Joel started his career at Unilever.
- Joel has an MBA from the University of Chicago, with concentrations in Economics and Statistics.
- Joel is a widely read blogger, published author and frequent speaker.
- Joel teaches Social Media Strategy at NYU Stern School of Business.

Email : **joel@rubinsonpartners.com** to design measurement approaches that will equip your organization to make the right calls today about our digital, social, and mobile marketing future.

RUBINSON PARTNERS, INC. GAME CHANGING ASSIGNMENTS

CONSUMER UNDERSTANDING

BRAND GUIDANCE

INNOVATION

Next Generation Marketing Mix Modelling

RPI has created approaches for improved estimation of digital and social media impact.

Reinventing Brand Tracking

Created a next generation approach that leverages social, digital data with survey and mobile research.

Sense, Respond, Anticipate

Designed one of the most comprehensive shopper insights listening and digital sensing platforms ever created in CPG.

Measurable Model of Media in a Paid, Owned, and Earned World

Created the first contemporary measurable model of media for large CPG marketers.

Path to Purchase Research

Conducted study on media's influence on shopper actions, not just awareness and intention.

Social Sharing Behaviors

Led one of the largest analyses of sharing behavior for ShareThis and SMG.

Value of a Facebook Fan

With Compete, determined the value of a Facebook fan is real but only if they return visits to the fan page.

Innovating Innovation

With InsightsNow, Inc. RPI offers an award winning system called BehaviorLens™ based on moments marketing.

Reinventing Smartphone Content and Advertising

For AOL, consulted on award winning project to understand smart phone owners' usage and motivations, published in HBR.

"Joel Rubinson is one of the greatest minds and innovators in the market research industry. He uniquely combines traditional experience and in-depth analytical skills with fresh thinking and creativity. He is a real problem solver and a pleasure to work with"

-Donna Goldfarb
Vice President, Consumer & Market Insights, Unilever, Americas

"Of all the partners with whom I regularly work, Joel brings a unique clarity to the challenges my organization is trying to solve. He has a command not only over the discipline of market research, but also how to frame the questions and the initiatives in a way that accelerate achieving the goal. This is what makes him such a rare breed of collaborator – in every interaction, I can count on Joel offering an honest and thoughtful assessment and a suggestion for a path forward."

-Christian Kugel
VP | Consumer Analytics & Research, AOL

"In my capacity as a global shopper insight manager I am always on the lookout for supplier partners who can add value to the debate. They are generally few and far between, but Joel was one of those. The discussions we had whilst Joel shaped the Synovate proposition for my business were stimulating and extremely useful – they were always business outcome focused. I do hope that I have the opportunity to work with Joel again in the future."

-Cliff McGregor
Global Shopper Insights Manager at Nestle

"I got to know Joel during our work together on the ARF, and I have been very impressed with his leadership, creativity and technical expertise. Joel has been the heart of the Research Transformation Initiative at the ARF, and he has brought fresh out of the box thinking, and a pro-activity and passion to the work that has resulted in unprecedented levels of industry participation and interest. I am looking forward to continuing to work with Joel in the future."

-Susan L. Wagner
Vice President, Global Strategic Insights

"Joel is a talented researcher and fortunately for us all, a very resourceful business partner. He knows his stuff, he knows nearly everybody in the business and he is constantly reaching to shape the future of marketing and insight."

-Michael Twitty
SVP, Strategic Planning and Insight
IN Marketing Services
(formerly head of shopper insights fur Unilever, Americas)

"Joel Rubinson has a great breadth of knowledge about the shopper marketing space, and is a terrific organizer and agent for progress on both the personal and group level. I have appreciated his initiative in ARF and Marketing Science sessions and in his personal assistance/guidance for some of my publications. He is a great team player with solid judgment."

-Herb Sorensen, PhD
Shopper Scientist LLC
(Founder, Sorensen Associates)

www.ingramcontent.com/pod-product-compliance
Lightning Source LLC
Chambersburg PA
CBHW050815180526
45159CB00004B/1680